URSA

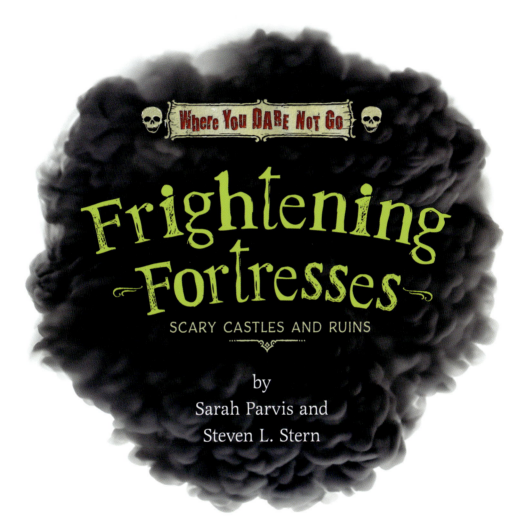

Where You DARE Not Go

Frightening Fortresses

SCARY CASTLES AND RUINS

by
Sarah Parvis and
Steven L. Stern

Minneapolis, Minnesota

Credits
Cover and title page, © Jason Reid/Adobe Stock and © faestock/Adobe Stock and © master1305/Adobe Stock; 4–5, © David/Adobe Stock and © FlexDreams/Adobe Stock and © NomadPhotoReference/Adobe Stock and © Passakorn Umpornmaha/Shutterstock; 6, © Abbas Al Yasiri/Shutterstock; 7TR, © Janzig/MiddleEast/Alamy Stock Photo; 7BR, © Pictures from History/Getty Images; 8, © tamas/Adobe Stock; 9, © Bearport Publishing; 10, © Caroline Brundle Bugge/iStock photo; 11BL, © Paula Jones/iStock photo; 12, © Calin Stan/Shutterstock; 13TR, © Public domain/Wikimedia; 13BL, © Pictures from History/Getty Images; 14, © WitR/Shutterstock; 15B, © Viktoras/Adobe Stock; 16, © Kev Gregory/Shutterstock; 17TR, © Classic Image/Alamy Stock Photo; 17BR, © Stefan/Adobe Stock; 18, © Wirestock Creators/Shutterstock; 19TR, © Public domain/Wikimedia; 19BL, © Astalor/iStock photo; 20, © jimmonkphotography/Shutterstock; 21MR, © Christine Matthews/geograph.org.uk; 22, © Dave0/Shutterstock; 23TR, © Duncan Savidge/Alamy Stock Photo; 24, © Public domain/Wikimedia; 25B, © Bearport Publishing; 26, © Ingo Bartussek/Shutterstock; 27B, © de Art/Adobe Stock; 28, © Hovaloft/Shutterstock; 29BL, © Gail Johnson/Shutterstock; 30, © Amy Nichole Harris/Shutterstock; 31TR, © Queso/iStock photo; 32, © Artur Sniezhyn/Shutterstock; 33TR, © National Portrait Gallery London/Wikimedia; 33BL, © Bettmann Archive/Getty Images; 34, © Medvedkov/iStock photo; 35TR, © Public domain/Wikimedia; 35BR, © John Keates/Alamy Stock Photo; 36, © TerryJLawrence/iStock photo; 37BR, © Ulia Koltyrina/Adobe Stock; 38, © Leonid Andronov/Shutterstock; 39TR, © Nora Yusuf/Shutterstock; 40, © Multishooter/Shutterstock; 41MR, © Thiago/Adobe Stock; 41BR, © Simon Annable/Alamy Stock Photo; 42–43, © Triff/Shutterstock

Bearport Publishing Company Product Development Team
Publisher: Jen Jenson; Director of Product Development: Spencer Brinker; Managing Editor: Allison Juda; Editor: Cole Nelson; Associate Editor: Naomi Reich; Associate Editor: Tiana Tran; Designer: Kim Jones; Designer: Kayla Eggert; Designer: Steve Scheluchin; Production Specialist: Owen Hamlin

Statement on Usage of Generative Artificial Intelligence
Bearport Publishing remains committed to publishing high-quality nonfiction books. Therefore, we restrict the use of generative AI to ensure accuracy of all text and visual components pertaining to a book's subject. See BearportPublishing.com for details.

Library of Congress Cataloging-in-Publication Data is available at www.loc.gov or upon request from the publisher.

ISBN: 979-8-89577-093-1 (hardcover)
ISBN: 979-8-89577-210-2 (ebook)

Copyright © 2026 Bearport Publishing Company. All rights reserved. No part of this publication may be reproduced in whole or in part, stored in any retrieval system, or transmitted in any form or by any means, electronic, mechanical, photocopying, recording, or otherwise, without written permission from the publisher. Bearport Publishing is a division of FlutterBee Education Group.

For more information, write to Bearport Publishing, 5357 Penn Avenue South, Minneapolis, MN 55419.

Contents

Frightening Ruins 4
Dying for Their Ruler 6
Hidden Room of Death 8
The Lost City 10
The Bloodthirsty Ruler 12
Human Hearts for the Sun God 14
A Murderous Marriage 16
The Hidden City of Tombs 18
A Phantom Prankster 20
The Ring of Stones 22
The Wailing Rocks 24
Bloody Rituals in the Jungle 26
The Blue Boy 28
The Stone Giants 30
The Headless Queen 32
Victims for the God of Rain 34
A Watery Grave 36
Strange Figures in the Desert 38
A Museum Mystery 40

A World Full of . . . Frightening Fortresses 42
Glossary 44
Read More 46
Learn More Online 46
Index 47

Frightening Ruins

Towering stone walls still stand strong around once-majestic castles and formerly solid forts. Abandoned stone monuments, huge carvings, and uncovered tombs sit crumbling in long-forgotten sacred spots. What do these places have in common? Unanswered questions about their mysterious—and sometimes bloody—pasts. And, perhaps, a wandering ghost or two. . . .

Dying for Their Ruler

UR
IRAQ

Ur was one of the world's earliest cities—thriving about 5,000 years ago. It was located in the region of Sumer (SOO-muhr), in what is now Iraq. A giant pyramid called a ziggurat, rose up from the center of the city. The impressive structure was built as a temple for the moon god, Nanna. Not far from the temple was Ur's royal burial ground. Unfortunately, when a ruler was laid to rest there, others from the city were killed and buried there as well.

The temple built for the moon god, Nanna

In the 1920s, British archaeologist Leonard Woolley discovered Ur's royal burial ground. He found the corpses of Sumerian kings and queens in these rooms carved out deep in the ground.

Ur's royal burial ground

The graves contained beautiful works of art as well as many silver and gold objects. They also revealed some disturbing facts about Sumerian rituals.

Close by the kings and queens lay the skeletons of their servants, soldiers, and musicians. Some rulers had been buried with more than 70 royal attendants. Many of them were young, and near each one was a gold or clay cup. The cups had been filled with a poisonous liquid. After the attendants had finished their deadly drink, they lay down to be buried with their ruler.

Proper burial was important to the Sumerians. They believed that the ghost of a person who had not been buried would haunt the living.

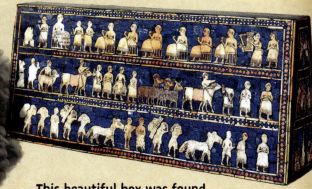

This beautiful box was found in the royal burial ground.

Hidden Room of Death

LEAP CASTLE
COUNTY OFFALY, IRELAND

The powerful O'Carroll clan lived at Leap Castle in the 1500s. These fierce fighters were often at war with other families. Many of their prisoners were killed in the castle's deadly dungeon. How exactly did they die? A fire would reveal the answer hundreds of years later.

Leap Castle

In 1922, a fire destroyed much of Leap Castle. As workers were cleaning up after the blaze, they made a terrifying discovery. Hidden beneath one of the floors was a secret dungeon. Sharp spikes came up from the stone floor. Hundreds of skeletons were still piled up inside.

To whom did the bones belong? Some were prisoners that the O'Carrolls had captured. Others were men hired to fight for the bloodthirsty clan. The O'Carrolls decided it was cheaper to murder the men after they were done fighting than to pay them. So, they just threw them into the dungeon.

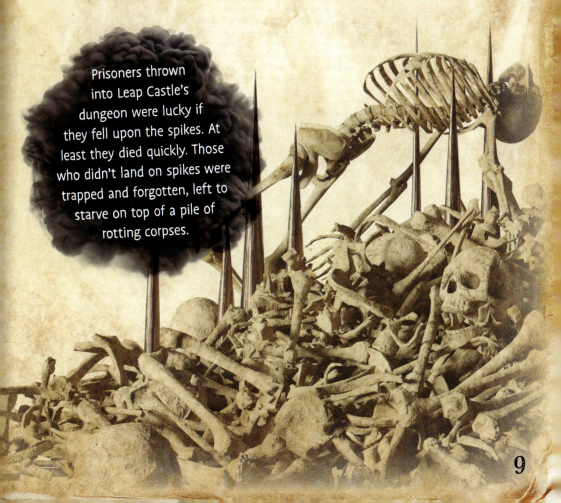

Prisoners thrown into Leap Castle's dungeon were lucky if they fell upon the spikes. At least they died quickly. Those who didn't land on spikes were trapped and forgotten, left to starve on top of a pile of rotting corpses.

The Lost City

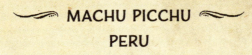

MACHU PICCHU

PERU

The Inca were the most powerful people in South America during the 1400s. Their massive empire stretched some 2,500 miles (4,000 km) from the present-day country of Ecuador to present-day Chile. After Spanish soldiers conquered the Inca in 1532, they destroyed many beautiful Incan buildings. Yet, one of the most splendid cities, Machu Picchu (MAH-choo PEE-choo), remained safe, hidden high on a mountaintop. Would it ever be found again?

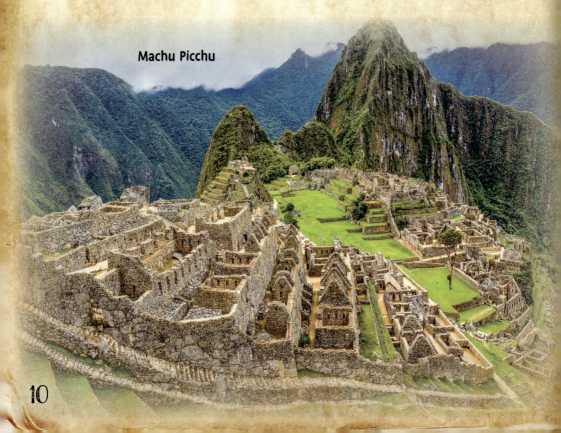

Machu Picchu

In 1911, American explorer Hiram Bingham set off for Peru to study Incan ruins. A villager told him of a secret city high up in the Andes Mountains. Was the story true? To find out, Bingham climbed up a steep mountainside covered by thick jungle. When he finally reached the top, 8,000 feet (2,400 m) up, he was amazed by what he saw.

Before him was a city that had been hidden from the outside world for almost 400 years. Poking through the clouds were about 200 buildings, including temples, palaces, and houses. Heavy blocks of gray granite had been perfectly cut to create these structures. Yet the Inca had no wheeled carts or iron tools. How could they have moved and shaped such large stones?

There was another puzzling question. What had happened to the people of Machu Picchu? Had they all been killed by another tribe, or did they die of some disease? The answer is as hard to find as the city itself.

The Intihuatana stone

The Intihuatana is a sacred stone at Machu Picchu dedicated to the Incan sun god. According to legend, some people could connect with the spirit world by touching their foreheads to the stone.

The Bloodthirsty Ruler

POIENARI CASTLE
WALLACHIA, ROMANIA

Prince Vlad III had an unusual way of murdering his enemies. He pierced them with a sharp pole. The poles were then planted in the ground and the victims would hang in the air, slowly dying from their wounds. Anyone who came across the impaled bodies would think twice about challenging the cruel ruler, who soon came to be known as Vlad the Impaler.

Poienari Castle

Vlad the Impaler became prince of Wallachia, which is part of modern-day Romania, in 1436. He needed a strong castle to stay safe from enemies and thought he had found a building that would be nearly impossible to attack—Poienari Castle. It was an ancient fortress located on a steep cliff. There was one problem, however. The castle lay in ruins. Prince Vlad would need many men to rebuild it, but he knew just whom to use.

Vlad the Impaler

Vlad's father and brother had been murdered in 1447. The noblemen who were supposed to defend his family had done nothing to save them. As punishment, Prince Vlad rounded up their families and forced them to hike more than 50 miles (80 km) to his new castle. Those who survived the journey were forced to carry huge rocks for the castle walls. Many were worked to death. Those who still lived were rewarded with a slow and painful death. Vlad impaled them on stakes around the castle.

Vlad's father was called Vlad Dracul, which means Vlad the dragon in Romanian. Prince Vlad was called Vlad Dracula, which means Vlad, son of the dragon. Prince Vlad may have been the inspiration for the vampire in Bram Stoker's famous novel Dracula.

Human Hearts for the Sun God

TENOCHTITLÁN
MEXICO

In the 1400s and early 1500s, the Aztec people had a vast empire in what is today Mexico. Its capital was Tenochtitlán (*tay*-nohch-TEET-lahn). Spanish soldiers, led by Hernán Cortés, conquered the Aztecs in 1521. They built what is now Mexico City over the ruins of Tenochtitlán. Yet even today, there are grim reminders of the Aztecs' bloody past.

Remains of Tenochtitlán

After sacrificing their victims, Aztec priests threw the bloody bodies off the pyramid. Then, the heads were cut off and stuck onto a *tzompantli*, or skull rack.

The splendid city of Tenochtitlán was built on an island in Lake Texcoco. There were white stone palaces along with temples, houses, and gardens. Most main streets were made of canals that people traveled by canoe. In the heart of the city stood the Templo Mayor. This building was about 90 ft. (30 m) tall, and at its top were twin temples, which honored two Aztec gods.

The city was beautiful, but it had a dark side. Each year, Aztec priests sacrificed thousands of people to win the favor of their sun god, Huitzilopochtli (*wee*-tsee-loh-POHCH-tlee). The victims, mostly prisoners of war, were led to the top of Huitzilopochtli's pyramid. There, the priests would cut out their still-beating hearts! When Cortés first came to Tenochtitlán in 1519, he told one of his men to count the skulls of recent victims. The man claimed to have counted 136,000 skulls!

A wall of carved skulls at the Templo Mayor

A Murderous Marriage

CASTLE RISING
NORFOLK, ENGLAND

What happens when a queen is imprisoned in her own castle? Does she lose her mind? Does she turn into a ghostly wolf after her death? Or does she do both?

Castle Rising

Queen Isabella was only about 12 years old in 1308 when she married King Edward II of England. Together, they had a son, Edward III, but it was not a marriage that would last. After 17 years, Queen Isabella fell in love with Roger Mortimer. Together, they gathered up an army, captured King Edward II, and had him killed on September 21, 1327.

Queen Isabella

Edward III became the new king, and according to some, he let his mother live the rest of her life in peace. Others, however, tell a darker tale. They believe Edward III punished Isabella by sending her away to Castle Rising, where she spent almost 30 years locked away from the world. Some stories say she lost her mind during this time. To this day, some visitors to Castle Rising have heard her crazed laughter echoing through the courtyards, while others have even seen her ghost. They say it takes the form of a giant white wolf with bloody fangs and fiery red eyes.

Queen Isabella may not be the only noisy ghost in the family. The ghost of King Edward II is heard every year on the day of his murder. His piercing screams are said to fill the hallways of the castle where he was killed.

The Hidden City of Tombs

PETRA
JORDAN

More than 2,000 years ago, the Nabataean people settled in Petra (PEE-truh), a desert city surrounded by mountains. Petra became a trade center and home to more than 20,000 people. Over time, however, trade routes changed, the city became less important, and the Nabataeans moved away. Petra was all but forgotten for more than 500 years, with no one but the region's Bedouin people setting eyes on the mysterious city.

An area of Petra

In 1812, Swiss explorer Johann Ludwig Burckhardt was traveling to Cairo and heard rumors of an ancient city lost in the desert sand and hidden from sight by mountains. Wondering if the rumors could be true, Burckhardt paid two Bedouin guides to lead him there. They took him to a long, narrow pass between towering rock walls. When Burckhardt stepped out into the sunlight on the other side, he was stunned.

Johann Ludwig Burckhardt

Pale red sandstone cliffs surrounded him. Carved into the cliffs were tombs, temples, burial chambers, and theaters. The Nabataeans had created these beautiful structures about 2,000 years before. Some of the carved tombs honored their gods, while others were built to remember the dead. The most surprising, however, were tombs for criminals—where they had been buried alive!

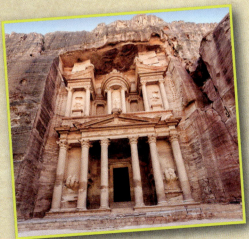

Tombs carved into the cliffs of Petra

About 400,000 people visit Petra each year. The site has even been used as a movie set. Yet even today, the only way to enter the hidden city is by foot, horse, or camel.

A Phantom Prankster

MUNCASTER CASTLE
CUMBRIA, ENGLAND

Kings, queens, and other powerful people in the past had servants to do everything for them. They had cooks to prepare food, messengers to carry letters, and even a person whose job was to make them laugh! This court jester—or fool—would juggle, dance, tell jokes, and play pranks. At Muncaster Castle, one court jester kept playing tricks even after he died.

Muncaster Castle

Archaeologist Clifford Jones went to Muncaster Castle in 2002 to look for ancient Roman coins and pottery. Instead, he found the ghost of Tom Fool—a court jester who lived about 400 years ago.

Tom was an expert at playing tricks on people. Sometimes, travelers would come to the castle and ask for directions to London. If Tom did not like them, he would point them away from the city and toward deadly quicksand. Who knows how many travelers were buried alive because of Tom's wicked jokes?

The tree where Tom Fool would play tricks on visitors

Some people, including Clifford Jones, believe that Tom continues to make mischief from beyond the grave. One night, Jones heard eerie chopping sounds in the empty castle. When he asked Tom's ghost to stop, it was suddenly quiet. A moment later, a light bulb above him exploded. Jones turned the corner and another bulb blew up. Everywhere he went, the lights shattered until Jones fled the castle.

Tom Fool was the court jester for Sir Pennington, who was known to be cruel. Pennington wanted to punish a man for falling in love with his daughter. So, he ordered Tom to murder the young man. Tom did it by cutting off his head.

The Ring of Stones

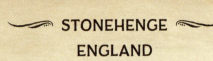

STONEHENGE
ENGLAND

On a misty plain in southern England stands an eerie sight. Huge gray stones, some weighing 25 tons (23 t), are arranged in a circle. The towering stone monument, called Stonehenge, was built by people who lived in the area thousands of years ago. What drove these ancient people to undertake such a difficult task? That is just one of the many mysteries surrounding Stonehenge.

Stonehenge

Around 3100 BCE, people in southern England began building an unusual monument. They brought gigantic stones, some from up to 240 miles (390 km) away, and arranged them upright in a circle. The work was slow and done in stages over 1,500 years. What were the people trying to build? No one knows for sure.

An arrangement of stones at the monument

Some people believe Stonehenge was built as a temple where people came for religious ceremonies. Others think it was used as an observatory to look at the sun, moon, and stars. Or it may have had other purposes. . . .

Sick and injured people may have traveled to Stonehenge, believing that the huge stones had magical healing powers. Others may have come to connect with the spirits of the dead. Some say that on quiet evenings, the murmurs of spirits from the past can still be heard.

Recent evidence indicates that Stonehenge was an ancient burial ground. It is estimated that as many as 240 people are buried there. This would make it the largest known cemetery of its time in England.

23

The Wailing Rocks

HACHIOJI CASTLE
TOKYO, JAPAN

Castles often had large armies to protect the men and women living inside. A tricky enemy, however, might wait to attack until an army was not around. What could the helpless people trapped inside do? More than 400 years ago, the Japanese women living at Hachioji Castle found out the sad answer.

A reconstructed entrance to Hachioji Castle

Hachioji Castle was built by the Japanese warrior Hojo Ujiteru in 1570, but it stood for just 20 years before tragedy struck. On June 23, 1590, an army of fierce samurai led by Lord Toyotomi Hideyoshi attacked the castle. Unfortunately, there weren't many warriors to defend the building as most of Hojo Ujiteru's forces were away fighting elsewhere. The women who remained at the castle knew they would not be safe for long.

To avoid being captured and tortured, the women within the fortress jumped to their deaths from the top of Hachioji Castle. It is said that their bodies created waterfalls of blood on the rocks below. The samurai destroyed much of the castle that day, and since then, it has remained abandoned, haunted by the doomed women. Visitors to the ruins report hearing the spine-chilling screams of women. They also hear the sickening thuds of bodies hitting the rocks.

According to Japanese legends, the ghosts of people who were murdered or who killed themselves are not able to rest peacefully. They remain on Earth seeking revenge. People should be very careful if they leave their homes between 2:00 and 3:00 a.m.— the time when the ghosts are most active.

Bloody Rituals in the Jungle

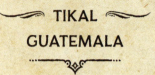

TIKAL
GUATEMALA

In 1848, explorers working for the Guatemalan government hacked their way through the tropical jungle. Spider monkeys danced in the trees, and jaguars hid in the green shadows. Suddenly, the explorers saw the top of a tall stone structure poking through the trees. They had found the ruins of the once-great Mayan city of Tikal (tee-KAHL).

Tikal

The Maya played a soccer-like ball game as part of their religious rituals. The cost of losing the game could be high. After some games, losers had their heads cut off as a sacrifice to the gods.

From about 250 CE to about 900 CE, the Maya had a great civilization in Central America and Mexico. They created beautiful buildings and works of art. They studied the stars and planets and also developed an advanced writing system and a yearly calendar.

At the center of this world was Tikal—a city of temples, palaces, and giant stone pyramids. It was here that the Maya also carried out their sacred rituals, killing turkeys, dogs, and other animals to win the favor of their gods. Even more terrifying, the Maya also sacrificed humans, taking the lives of prisoners, people who were enslaved, and sometimes even children.

About 1,300 years ago, more than 50,000 people lived in Tikal and the surrounding areas. By the end of the tenth century, however, the city had mysteriously become a ghost town. Before long, the jungle covered Tikal, hiding its bloody secrets.

The Blue Boy

CHILLINGHAM CASTLE
NORTHUMBERLAND, ENGLAND

During the 1200s, up to 50 people a week were tortured at Chillingham Castle. So it's no surprise that this building is said to be haunted by its bloody past. One of its most well-known ghosts is the mysterious Blue Boy.

Chillingham Castle

Chillingham Castle was built in the 1100s. Today, tourists can stay overnight in some parts of the haunted building; but beware of sleeping in the Pink Room! That is where the ghostly Blue Boy appears.

Those who have slept in the Pink Room say the Blue Boy shows up at midnight. At that hour, they hear a blood-curdling wail that sounds like the awful cry of a child in great pain. When the startled guests look up, the image of a boy dressed in blue appears, surrounded by a glowing light. The ghost stays for a moment, then floats toward the fireplace and disappears through a wall.

In the 1920s, bones and scraps of blue clothing were found hidden behind the wall where the ghostly boy vanishes. Perhaps they belonged to him. The bones were given a proper burial in hopes of finally giving the boy's spirit some rest. But so far it hasn't worked. . . .

A re-creation of a prisoner being tortured

In the torture room at Chillingham, victims were boiled in pots and locked in cages with starving rats. Some prisoners were rolled inside barrels full of spikes or stretched on a rack. The floor of this scary room is tilted so that blood can drain away. Even today, tour guides are afraid to enter the creepy torture chamber alone.

The Stone Giants

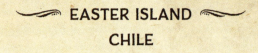

EASTER ISLAND
CHILE

Easter Island is one of the most out-of-the-way places on Earth. It is located far out in the South Pacific Ocean, about 2,180 miles (3,500 km) west of Chile. The island is only about 63 square miles (163 sq km), about the size of Washington, D.C. Yet somehow hundreds of stone giants began appearing on the island around 1,000 years ago. How did they get there?

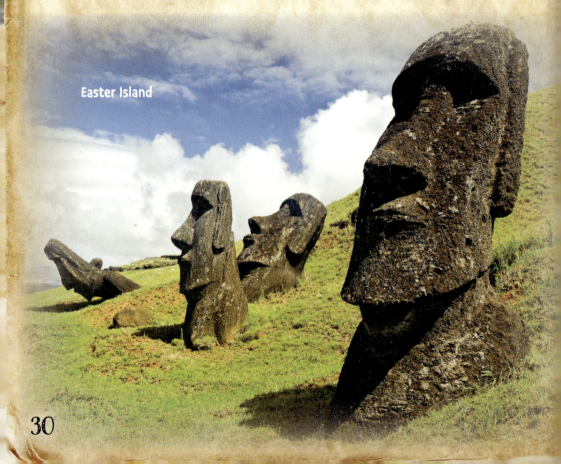

Easter Island

When the first Europeans landed on Easter Island in the 1700s, what they saw stopped them in their tracks. Hundreds of frightening stone statues stared down at them. Some were more than 30 ft. (9 m) tall and weighed more than 80 tn. (73 t).

Easter Island *moai*

Between about 1200 and 1650, ancient Polynesian people carved more than 800 statues to honor their ancestors. These statues were called *moai* (mo-EYE). Using only simple tools, the Easter Islanders somehow were able to create the giant *moai* and move them onto great stone platforms.

War between groups of islanders broke out around 1680. Attacks grew more and more bloody, with some groups even eating their dead enemies. The islanders tried to destroy one another's *moai*, and by the early 1800s, nearly all the statues had been knocked down. More than 100 years later, archaeologists raised some of the fallen statues. Today, these stone giants once again watch over Easter Island.

Some people think the statues are too big and heavy to have been made by ancient people. They believe that the islanders must have had help—from beings not of Earth! In fact, the huge statues are so strange-looking that some people say they are sculptures of robots made by space aliens.

The Headless Queen

TOWER OF LONDON
LONDON, ENGLAND

The Tower of London has been used as both a fortress and a home to England's kings and queens. It also served as a famous jail. For hundreds of years, prisoners at the Tower of London were tortured, beheaded, hanged, and burned at the stake. With so many violent deaths, it's no wonder that some say the Tower is the most haunted castle in England.

The Tower of London

King Henry VIII married his second wife, Anne Boleyn, in 1533. They lived together at the Tower of London. King Henry hoped they would have a son who would become king after him. When his wife did not have a boy, King Henry began to lose interest in her and wanted to marry another woman who would give him a son. So in 1536, he imprisoned Anne in the Tower and sentenced her to death.

Anne Boleyn

On May 19, 1536, Anne stepped onto a small platform on the Tower's lawn. She gave a short speech before kneeling down. A blindfold was tied around her face so she could not see what was coming next. With one blow, a swordsman sliced off her head. She was then buried in an unmarked grave.

Yet some people say the queen can still be seen. Her headless ghost is said to roam around the Tower, frightening workers and visitors. Sometimes, she even carries her head in her arms as she wanders.

Anne Boleyn about to be killed

Anne Boleyn was lucky to be killed with a sword. Most beheadings took place with an axe. If the axe was not sharp enough or if the executioner had poor aim, the victim would not die instantly. In 1541, Margaret Pole, the Countess of Salisbury, was struck many times with an axe before she died.

Victims for the God of Rain

CHICHÉN ITZÁ
MEXICO

In southeastern Mexico stand the ruins of Chichén Itzá (chee-CHEN eet-SAH). Stone temples, pyramids, and other buildings offer clues about the people who lived there more than 1,000 years ago. Many chilling stories are told about the city. Are they fact or fiction? The bones of the city's victims may tell the tale.

Chichén Itzá

Archaeologists do not all agree on Chichén Itzá's history. They know that the city was part of the Maya civilization, but other ancient peoples, such as the powerful Toltecs, may also have lived there. What archaeologists do agree on is that Chichén Itzá was a sacred place . . . and a city of death.

Inside the city of Chichén Itzá was the sacred well, or *cenote* (sin-OH-tee). This round cavern was about 210 ft. (65 m) wide and 110 ft. (34 m) deep. No one drank the water, however. Instead, people came here to make offerings to Chac, the god of rain and lightning.

A statue of Chac

Water was scarce, and people needed rain to grow crops. So, they offered Chac gold, copper, and jade—in addition to human sacrifices! The living victims were thrown into the well. When archaeologists excavated the well, they found hundreds of bones, many of which were from the skeletons of children.

The Maya believed that the dead went down to a dark underworld called Xibalba. The *cenote* was a gateway to this underworld.

The sacred well

35

A Watery Grave

SCOTNEY CASTLE
KENT, ENGLAND

One way to keep a castle safe was to build a moat around it. This deep ditch filled with water made it very difficult for attackers to reach the people in the castle. Many castles had moats, but some were said to be the home of ghosts!

Scotney Castle

Scotney Castle, built in the 1300s, is located in Kent, England. In the 1700s, England was home to many smugglers. Some sold illegal items, while others sold things without paying taxes to the king. These smugglers had to be careful. If they were caught, they could be imprisoned and killed.

Arthur Darell owned Scotney Castle in the early 1700s. It is said that he was a smuggler and probably a murderer, too. According to local stories, when an officer discovered that Darell was a smuggler, the two men began to fight. Darell killed the officer and dumped the body into the moat at Scotney Castle so he would not be caught. Ever since, people have reported seeing a dripping wet ghost crawling out of the water. It limps slowly to the castle and bangs on the door, but no sounds can be heard. Then, the figure disappears into thin air.

Some think Arthur Darell faked his own death in 1720 so no one would know he was smuggling. It is said that at Darell's funeral, a man in a long black coat appeared. Someone heard this stranger whisper, "That is me they think they are burying." Moments later, the man was gone. Was this Darell, or was it his ghost?

Strange Figures in the Desert

NAZCA
PERU

When airplanes first began flying over the Peruvian desert in the 1920s, people aboard looked down and gasped. Far below, carved into the dry soil, were hundreds of lines and figures. Who made these amazing drawings? Gods? Aliens? Giants?

Drawings found at Nazca

Soon, scientists came to the Peruvian desert to investigate the mysterious drawings. They found hundreds of lines and pictures. Someone had created the drawings by scraping away reddish-brown desert stones to expose the yellow soil underneath. There were pictures of birds, a spider, and even a monkey. Each of the images was gigantic. One drawing of a lizard was bigger than two soccer fields put together!

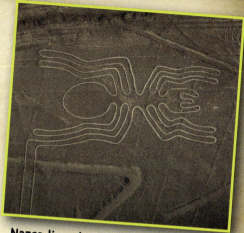
Nazca lines in the shape of a spider

About 2,000 years ago, the Nazca (NAHS-kuh) people lived in this desert area. Could they have carved these figures? If so, why would they make them so large that they could be clearly seen only from above?

Among the pictures of animals and plants, scientists also found images of strange beings. One figure had two huge hands—one of which had only four fingers. Another figure, about 100 ft. (30 m) tall, looked like a man with huge eyes. Is it possible that these were drawings of creatures that had visited Earth in the time of the Nazca?

Some people believe that the drawings are landing strips for returning aliens. Why else can they be seen only from the sky?

A Museum Mystery

TAMWORTH CASTLE
STAFFORDSHIRE, ENGLAND

Tamworth Castle, part of which is now a museum, was built in the late 1000s. Today, tourists can visit different parts of the building, including its dungeon and a haunted bedroom. The men and women who work at Tamworth say ghostly figures are often spotted around the castle. Sounds sometimes come from empty rooms. Workers have even seen—and felt—things that they cannot explain.

Tamworth Castle

In the 1990s, a museum worker named June Hall was preparing an exhibit for the castle called "The Tamworth Story." When she opened up the exhibition room one morning, she felt as if sand had been thrown in her face.

For a moment, Hall was blinded. She then looked down, thinking she would be covered in dirt, but her clothes were clean. Val Lee, another member of the staff, entered the room just then and saw Hall bent over, rubbing her eyes. When they both looked up, they did not see a person. Instead, they saw a swirl of blue mist about 6 ft. (2 m) tall. Then, as quickly as it had appeared, the mist was gone.

Neither Hall nor Lee knows what could have caused these spooky events. Was it one of the many ghosts that live at Tamworth Castle?

How often do people experience ghostly activity at Tamworth Castle? According to one of the workers at the castle, a day doesn't go by without something happening that she can't explain.

A bedroom in Tamworth Castle

A World Full of...

PACIFIC OCEAN

NORTH AMERICA

Ghostly sacrifices in Tenochtitlán, Mexico

A sacred well in Chichén Itzá, Mexico

ATLANTIC OCEAN

Mysterious drawings in Nazca, Peru

An abandoned city in Tikal, Guatemala

SOUTH AMERICA

Stone giants on Easter Island, Chile

The forgotten city of Machu Picchu, Peru

SOUTHERN OCEAN

42

Frightening Fortresses

Glossary

abandoned left empty; no longer used

aliens creatures from outer space

ancestors family members who lived a long time ago

ancient very old

archaeologist a scientist who learns about ancient times by studying artifacts, such as old buildings, tools, and pottery

attendants servants

Bedouin Arab people of the desert regions of the Middle East

beheaded had one's head chopped off

bloodthirsty eager for violence and death

burial ground an area of land where dead bodies are buried

canals human-made waterways for boats

clan a large family or group of families with a single leader

corpses dead bodies

court jester a person whose job was to entertain kings, queens, and nobles

dungeon a dark prison cell, usually underground

excavated uncovered by digging

executioner a person whose job is to kill prisoners

exhibit a presentation or display

fierce violently hostile

graves holes dug into the ground where dead people are buried

impaled killed by being stabbed with a sharp pole

jade a green stone used for making jewelry and ornaments

legend a story handed down from long ago that is often based on some facts but cannot be proved true

mischief playing pranks or doing things to annoy others

moat a wide ditch dug around a palace or castle that is filled with water

monument a structure built to honor a person or event

observatory a place or building for viewing stars and planets

offering something given or sacrificed, usually to a god or gods

Polynesian relating to islands in the Pacific Ocean

pyramids stone monuments with square bases and triangular sides that meet at a point on top

quicksand wet, loose sand that someone can sink into and become stuck

rituals special ceremonies for religious or other purposes

ruins what is left of something that has decayed or been destroyed

sacred holy, religious

sacrificed killed a person or animal as part of a ceremony or as an offering to a god

samurai Japanese warriors, or soldiers, who lived in medieval times (400 CE–1500 CE)

smugglers people who secretly move goods in or out of a country in a way that is against the law

spirit a supernatural creature, such as a ghost

splendid beautiful, shining, or brilliant in appearance

stakes strong sticks or poles with pointed ends

taxes money people pay to support the government

temple a religious building where people worship

Toltecs people of a Native American empire in Mexico that existed from the 900s through the 1100s

tombs rooms or buildings for the dead

torture chamber a room where someone causes great pain to another

tragedy a terrible event that causes great sadness or suffering

vampire in stories, a dead person who rises from the grave to suck the blood of people

45

Read More

Brinker, Spencer and Stuart Webb. *Phantoms Among Us: Ghosts, Spirits, and Spectral Hauntings (The Unexplained).* Minneapolis: Bearport Publishing Company, 2025.

Hansen, Grace. *History's Spookiest Paranormal Events (History's Greatest Mysteries).* Minneapolis: ABDO, 2023.

Sheen, Barbara. *Ghosts and Spirits (Exploring the Occult).* San Diego: ReferencePoint Press, 2024.

Williams, Dinah. *Horror Healing: Scary Hospitals and Asylums (Where You Dare Not Go).* Minneapolis: Bearport Publishing Company, 2025.

Learn More Online

1. Go to **FactSurfer.com** or scan the QR code below.
2. Enter "**Frightening Fortresses**" into the search box.
3. Click on the cover of this book to see a list of websites.

Index

Aztec 14-15
Bedouins 18-19
Bingham, Hiram 11
Blue Boy 28-29, 43
Boleyn, Anne 33
Burckhardt, Johann Ludwig 19
Castle Rising 16-17
cenote 35
Chac 35
Chichén Itzá, Mexico 34-35, 42
Chillingham Castle 28-29
Cortés, Hernán 14-15
court jester 20-21
Darell, Arthur 37
Dracula 13
Easter Island, Chile 30-31, 42
Edward II, King 17
ghosts 25, 28, 36, 41
Hachioji Castle 24-25
Henry VIII, King 33
Inca 10-11
Isabella, Queen 17
Jones, Clifford 21
Leap Castle 8-9
Machu Picchu, Peru 10-11, 42
Maya 26-27, 35
moai 31
moat 36-37
Mortimer, Roger 17
Muncaster Castle 20-21
murder 9, 17, 21

Nabataeans 18-19
Nazca, Peru 38-39, 42
O'Carroll clan 8
Petra, Jordan 18-19, 43
Poienari Castle 12-13
Pole, Margaret 33
prisoners 8-9, 15, 27, 29, 32, 43
sacrifices 35, 42
samurai 25
Scotney Castle 36-37
smugglers 37
Stoker, Bram 13
Stonehenge, England 22-23, 43
Sumer 6
Tamworth Castle 40-41
Tenochtitlán, Mexico 14-15, 42
Tikal, Guatemala 26-27, 42
Toltecs 35
Tom Fool 21
torture chamber 29
Tower of London 32-33
Ur, Iraq 6-7, 43
vampire 13
Vlad the Impaler 12-13
Woolley, Leonard 7
ziggurat 6

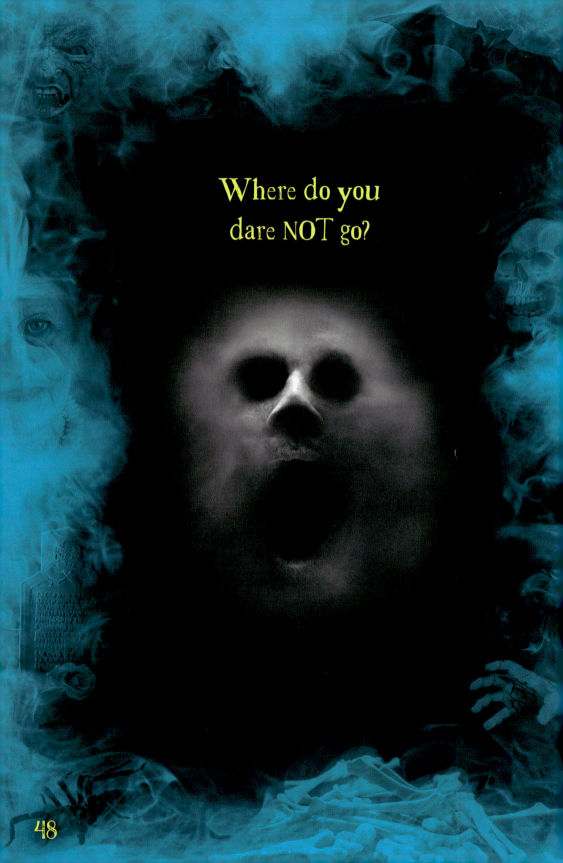